The

TELEPHONE
ASSASSIN

Everything you need to know about being **successful** on the phone

ANTHONY STEARS

First published in Great Britain in 2013 by Anthony J Stears

© Anthony J Stears 2013 All rights reserved

Published by Telephone Assassin Ltd

A CIP Catalogue record for this book is available from the British Library.

The moral rights of the author have been asserted.

Design by www.ebook-designs.co.uk

Printed in Great Britain by Lulu

DEDICATION & THANKS

This book and everything I have achieved wouldn't have been possible without the support of a handful of people, so I'd like to dedicate this:

To my father, the man on a pedestal, with shoes too big to fill. Always encouraging me to do what I love, your on-going support has turned that cheeky, dyslexic, minimalist into a proud author.

To my mum, for believing I could do anything I set my mind to, your support has brought me through the toughest times.

To Phil Jones, mentor and friend, your recognition and support gave me the courage to stand alone and do what I do best. It was you that urged me to write this book, and with Steph onside ready to offer a helping hand, I am truly grateful for your encouragement and support.

To Tim Rees for your continued support as a client and for encouraging me to use the "Telephone Assassin" name.

And most important of all, Carly. The love of my life, my entire world. You are the only one who can pick me up when I'm down, make me smile when I'm sad, make me cry with happiness and give me the kick up the backside I sometimes need. Without your support this book wouldn't have ever got finished.

Thank you to all xx

CONTENTS

PREFACE

The reason for writing this book is because after 10 years generating leads for a huge selection of different businesses, I have managed to perfect the process to a point where I truly believe you can get anyone's attention in the business world, if you take the right approach.

I don't claim to be a sales or marketing expert, so it came as a bit of a shock when I found myself as the sales and marketing manager for 5 companies all at the same time. Charging money upfront I had to deliver week on week, so had to work out what worked and what didn't pretty quickly.

At the same time I was managing to play golf once a week too, and I tell people this not because I'm any good at golf (I'm not), but simply because for most businesses just 2-4 hours a week of the right activity, is all that's needed to make a huge difference. Here's the catch.... my process only works if you are good at what you do, so once you have "set out your stall properly" (created a professional presence and credibility), the principles and approach is much the same across all sectors and sizes of business. After attending an introduction to NLP and working closely with Tristan Soames (an NLP Master Trainer), I began to fully understand exactly how my communication style and optimistic mind-set helps me to build rapport so quickly over the phone, and that the process I've developed is simply a very effective method to cultivate profitable business relationships.

We need to stop people going backwards with their communication ability and stop them hiding behind technology all the time. With most of what I do initiated over the phone, I've managed to earn the nick-name 'The Telephone Assassin ', and believe I prove every day that some of the old fashioned ways are best.

We all hear people talking about "Connecting" and "Engaging" with people, yet many of us rely too much on automated services and blasting spam, or spending ages on social media looking for your next client, rather than just picking up the phone.

I've noticed that over the past few years the number of calls I receive on New Year's Eve has gone right down and the number of text messages has gone through the roof. Close friends and family members that used to call now text and it's sad that toneless messages are replacing great conversations and robbing us of great memories and interaction. It amazes me that many business owners appear to think that if they send enough email, post enough blogs and advertise in the right places that work will fall into their laps. We all want to get found on Google when people are searching, but without patience and deep pockets (or a very niched product or service), the only way to really connect with someone and establish a potential future need is by speaking with them.

With this in mind, many of us choose to spend lots of time and money trying to spread our net as far as it will go and get terrible conversion ratios, when in reality, a few simple phone calls will get a faster response and allow you to choose who you target. I appreciate that we all like the convenience of a one-stop-shop, however I would rather deal with a specialist offering quality and value any day.

Guilty of trying to help with everything myself, I found that I was working like crazy but had hit the limit of what I could do in the number of hours I had. Although it was a principle I used for my clients it was the wise words from my mentor Phil M Jones, that was "to own your niche", which really hit home for me. Basically, stick to what you're good at and become the expert and THE go-to person for that particular thing.

Anything in business is possible and you can get in front of anyone you want if you take the right approach.

SOME SUCCESSES STORIES -

Lanix - IT Support company
Business Development – Ad-hoc Sales and Marketing support

An introduction from an existing client lead me to meet Chris, the owner at Lanix Ltd based out of Isleworth. Our discussion quickly lead to a visit into the office to find out a bit more about what Lanix do and how I could help.

> *We had identified some key market segments we could target and the calls began, targeting high end cosmetic companies. It didn't take long before we were in front of a respected brand talking with the decision makers about how we could support them going forwards, as some future opportunities had been identified. Continuing on from this, on Anthony's 12th attempt to contact one of the biggest names in this sector, he proceeded to have a very positive conversation for 20 minutes with their IT Director (responsible for all their fashion stories across Europe) and got them to ask us, if we could support them in the roll-out of some new software they were looking to use. The software that this giant brand was about to start using is from one of the UK's top EPOS providers and a call from Anthony has led to several meetings and a partnership agreement has taken place. Further to this*

his persistence paid off once more leading us to form a consortium with one of the UK's top hardware providers and positioning ourselves as the go-to-people in this market."

"Anthony's ability to build rapport is fantastic, accompanying us on meetings and helping to train junior members of staff, he has proved a real asset and I can safely say that if you can come up with a wish list of clients, he can show you how to get in front of them."

Chris Kwok - Lanix Ltd

Working for one of the top office furniture companies in the world I worked with one of their resellers targeting a wish list of clients. Some clever "positioning" enabled me to get them in front of the head of Coca Cola's procurement department to conduct a survey to "help us understand what is important to them in the procurement process."

What a fantastic way to get in front of a potential client and being able to ask the questions that count. Finding out what is important (price, quality, service, speed of delivery, ext...) puts you in the perfect position to offer potential clients what they want, in the way that they want it.

Adveticus - Protective clothing

Awareness
4 days spread over a month!

The Objective
When we first approached MAD, our objective was simply to create Awareness at the highest level possible in some of the largest banks and insurance companies in the UK, without it costing the earth!

Project Description
Adveticus was a new company with a totally unique product (anti-viral respirators) and it was our goal to get some of the country's largest banks and insurance companies talking about us. From experience we found out just how hard it is to get to the highest people in these very large companies but Anthony took the time to fully understand our unique products and discuss the problems we were facing.

Results
At the end of every day he worked for us, Anthony discussed all the results from that day and everything we needed to do, like sending extra information or doing follow up calls. With some great results early on, on just the second day Anthony reported back on a very positive conversation he'd had with HSBC earlier that day, and true to his word that evening we were over the

moon to see that they had been all over our website. It even turned out that the chap we had been speaking to had recently given talks in the cabinet office on this particular topic!

> *If you're starting up or just struggling to make an impact, I would certainly recommend speaking with Anthony at Marketing and Data."*

Clare O'Connell - Director

Bespoke Investments - Property Investments

Data Cleansing and Enhancement
1-2 days a week for 3 months

Objective
When we first approached Anthony at MAD we were still in the early stages of establishing the business and both my business partner and I simply didn't have time to go through our huge amount of records we brought to the table. We simply needed someone to go through our old databases, getting rid of the deadwood and establishing which ones were "HOT" and still actively looking at investing.

Campaign Description

Dubious about having the calls off site I was keen on having the calls done from our own office and Anthony was more than happy to do this. Although he describes what he did for us as "data enhancement" Anthony's background and understanding in the property market meant we got a lot more than just someone sat on the phone checking details. In fact, he soon became a member of the team.

Results

Half way through the hour we had put aside for training on the first morning, I was interrupted by a phone call and not one to let the phones ring for too long I soon gave Anthony the nod to answer another call which was coming in. I was very reassuring to hear him selling our latest development opportunity to a potential investor in such a professional and confident way. We gave him a spreadsheet of contacts to work through and as well as qualifying investors for our central database, Anthony took more of an account managers role discussing and sending out details and following them up and passing them over to me to discuss procedures and seal the deal.

 I'd recommend Anthony without a second thought."

Tristan Soames - Director

Green Lane Solutions Ltd

Full Marketing Support
3 days per week ongoing

> *After sitting down with Anthony it was clear that he has drive and passion in abundance with a real can do attitude, so I decided to bring him into the office to learn a little more about what the company does and discuss where he feels he could help. A week later he came back with a full marketing break down including hints and tips for our website, and individual ideas tailored for each aspect of my business and how we could promote them and where we could open up potential new channels.*
>
> *With the focus being put on what would be most profitable we realised that if we had the ability to get to clients at a much earlier stage, we would be able to offer ALL of our services in one go and maximize each clients spend. Anthony's idea was to offer a unique service to commercial agents and somehow convince them to recommending us! Within a few weeks he not only arranged a meeting with one of Savills directors in London but he had also persuaded 15 commercial agents around London to start recommend us to suitable clients. Utilising our resources he was also able to get a handful of serviced office brokers to do the same.*

With this underway, we turned our efforts to the website and Anthony's knowledge of web promotion and SEO has allowed us to make the right changes ourselves and not only helped us to increase our profile but turned our website into a real asset to the business.

Anthony has only been working with us for the past 2 months but I look forward to moving on to the next campaign as he has already come up with great angles and will allow us to start building on our longer term contracts. I will continue working with MAD and would (and have) recommend him to anyone looking to grow their business.

Tim Rees - Managing Director

Select

Marketing Support
Ad-hoc as required

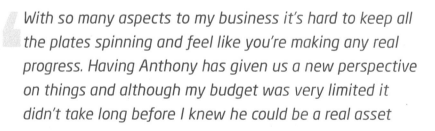

With so many aspects to my business it's hard to keep all the plates spinning and feel like you're making any real progress. Having Anthony has given us a new perspective on things and although my budget was very limited it didn't take long before I knew he could be a real asset

to my business. By breaking down the company into its various departments it was clear to see where the opportunities and weaknesses are, and a short discussion enabled us to put together a marketing plan which was more than achievable but also measurable.

With our own in-house photographer rarely going out and new mast equipment going unused I wanted to start by helping him to gain some momentum. Anthony highlighted that a lack of examples on the website probably wasn't helping, and came up with a plan to gain the opportunity to work on some fantastic local architecture. Including a couple of luxury Hotels and Golf courses and with permission to use them for examples on the website, it not only helped to us to start building a portfolio but boosted Ryan's confidence immensely. In under a month he set up 5 venues that were happy for us to use their shots for our website and as a result one of them has now started to spend money and others are asking us about our other printing services. I asked Anthony to come in and spend a couple of hours with Ryan (our photographer) to show him how to gain his own opportunities and how to get the most from each one, turning him into more of a salesman than just a photographer. Time well spent and I intend doing something similar with other members of staff (myself *included)*

Our website is obviously very important to our business but we've been stung in the past by optimisation companies and although we have great design abilities the site has never gained enough momentum to start generating revenue. Anthony explained (in simple terms) exactly how the internet and optimisation works and what the reasons and benefits are behind using things like Facebook and Twitter. Most importantly he has shown me how to monitor (and understand) the site so I can see exactly what is happening on a day-to-day and month-to-month basis. A little less intimidated by the web, I'm now confident that the small budget I have can now be spent on the right things.

Helping out in many areas of the business, it is great to have Anthony on hand as and when I need him. To call with new ideas or for a creative second opinion, even to have someone chasing me who will make sure that I too stick to and achieve my goals. With a positive can-do attitude, anything seems possible and Anthony's drive and passion is infectious and I would not hesitate for a second in recommending him to anyone looking to grow or develop their business.

David Cooper – Managing Director

ARE WE ALL PRODUCTS OF OUR ENVIRONMENT?

I always knew I would enjoy the world of business. Even from a young age my father spotted my entrepreneurial skills, especially when he realised I'd been making myself a tidy profit selling his prize possessions from the garage after seeing someone else having a "garage sale".

I had my list of chores to do to earn my pocket money as a kid, and quickly came up with ingenious ways to make things easier and for some time little did my dad know that I found the polishing and hoovering of the lounge so easy. It wasn't until I was caught red handed using the smallest of the nest of tables to drag marks/lines in to the carpet (which just so happen to be same size as the hoover), so killing two birds with one stone, dusted tables and carpet that looked vacuumed, Genius! To my surprise he actually couldn't stop laughing, saying I was a chip off the old block and he found it much funnier than trying to sell his tools and camping equipment in my "garage sale"! I didn't realise just how much I would look up to my dad and it's only as I've grown up that I've understood the massive impact his working career has had on the IT industry. I never had any interest in IT as a kid and always thought it was so technical that I would never understand, but learning about what he did as MD of Insignia Solutions back in the 80's and 90's leaves me in awe of him, and to find out he wasn't really technical at all, and it was all about "managing" changed my view. It was his passion and sense of reason that enabled him to sell the idea of an opportunity and cultivate great, long lasting relationships with staff and clients. His explanation of the 2 types of sales guys you need was simple, you have Hunters and Farmers. Farmers nurture the client and Hunters come in to close the deal. He was a farmer and I suppose that's what I am too, although I like to think I do it so well that the hunter can take a break, while I help them to buy. ☺

During my GCSE's I found it hard to decide exactly what I wanted to do with life and what career path I should choose. My mother and step-father owned a sheet metal factory and as a teenager I worked there at any opportunity, from weekends to entire summer holidays, as I was hungry for the experience from the shop floor up to the boardroom. I loved all aspects of the business, especially using some of the large machinery and some of the hand held tools that took such precision, boys and their toys! I loved wearing a boiler-suit that drowned me and singing along to the radio while trying not to get caught smoking rollies. I remember being assigned the huge task of looking after the dispatch department while someone was on holiday for 2 weeks, and was asked to have "a good sort out and tidy up". Within a few days I had a whole new system in place that was clean and tidy and worked brilliantly with a shop floor, with a clearly defined system. Even if it wasn't your job, you knew what had to be done and where things should go. That's when I realised how important "systems" and being organised were in the world of business.

When I selected my A-levels (maths, drama and business studies), I was unaware how well they would set me up perfectly for a life in sales. My wise business studies teacher, Mr. Higgins, was great and I can remember a conversation where he told me I needed to find a job that kept me interested, to which I made a cocky comment like, "yeah, something nice and easy, that pays well". He smiled and said, "it won't matter how much you earn, if you don't enjoy doing it, you will get bored and complacent."

Once I had decided on a sales role, I looked at what could produce the biggest commission. So, for my first taste of employment I just knew I wanted to sell houses, as this is one of the most expensive purchases of most people's lives and I figured if I can do this, I could sell anything! I went for three interviews and got offered all three jobs, but decided not to be greedy and took the job with the best training opportunities which unfortunately had the lowest pay, (just £8000 p.a). Starting at the bottom in one of the region's top offices, I was happy walking the streets leaflet dropping and sorting out the post at the end of every day, as I was able to see exactly how everything worked. Building your own customer base was key, so I was always the first to answer the phone, (often within half a ring), and this meant I got more new customers that anyone else. After nearly 4 years and lots of company awards, I decided it was time for a change of direction. I found out that my step father was terminally ill and he wanted my help at work and home, and I took this time with him to do anything he asked really. He sold the businesses and we made the most of the time we had together, with him teaching me all he could. This was a sad time for me, but it taught me that you need to work hard to get what you want out of life and the quicker the better, so you can have some time at the end to look back on all you've achieved.

I then joined Thompson Directories selling a data profiling tool that enabled businesses to filter down a database (for mailshots, telemarketing etc.), to include JUST their ideal clients, thus massively reducing the size and cost of their campaigns and making a ROI (return on investment), from just one sale. I had a great boss who had the ability to motivate everyone in the team and give the support when needed. I remember her lending me a couple of CD's of a motivational type speaker who talked about the psychology of communication and the power of our voice and body-language on others which I found fascinating.

I was so helpful to my clients, showing them ways of using the system without needing lots of credits that I rarely hit ALL of my targets, although I seemed to get a lot more referrals than everyone else and my call times were always above what they should be, (targets were 4 hours per day).

I then began helping clients with the direct mail pieces and writing telemarketing scripts for various situations from warm-up calls to qualification calls and follow-ups to closing calls. With enough clients asking me to make the calls for them I set up a telemarketing company call Marketing and Data Ltd (aka MAD) with a colleague from Thomson.

I got my fingers burnt by choosing the wrong business partners and learnt some very valuable lessons along the way. I was responsible for securing new business by winning clients over with a freebie, and doing the calls myself to prove that we can generate exactly what they're looking for. "Dave" my business partner, then managed the campaigns and staff and became their account manager. Although he was cheerful, enthusiastic and thick-skinned, he liked to exaggerate, and when this turned into lies and he began mis-selling, his lies caught up with him and came to bite us in the ass. A convenient spell of laryngitis meant he couldn't come in to work or even talk to me for 3 weeks and he swiftly left the company, leaving me to pick up the pieces. With wages to pay and £7k of expected revenue now not coming in, I felt the overwhelming responsibility towards the young team we had begun to build (many in their first proper job). After paying everyone what was owed and giving references to all the staff I decided to let them all go, move out of the serviced office (reducing overheads) and came to the conclusion that no-one was going to be able to do the calls quite like me or could be trusted to consistently deliver good results, so I need to work closer with my client going forwards.

I needed a break and managed to do some travelling through over 20 countries, learning to dive, jumping out of a plane, riding elephants, training tigers in a temple, hiked into active volcanos... and experienced culture like never before. It was humbling to see people with nothing (and I mean nothing), who were happy, smiling and kind. I learnt so much while I was away and despite leaving as a smart, clean shaven guy with short, dark spiky hair, I returned with a whole new attitude and a big curly hair do and beard.

Just a couple of years after my return I found myself as the sales and marketing manager for 5 companies, as I mentioned before. The reason I talk about playing golf at the same times as delivering week on week for all these clients, is because I believe sales really is just a part-time job and for most SME clients I've worked with, just a few hours every week of the right activity made all the difference.

With a growing waiting list of clients and no way to service them all, I began working with a NLP Master Trainer who helped me to analyse my processes and communication style, to help me understand how I was able to deliver such great results. This has enabled me to develop a selection of training workshops designed to help those people responsible for generating leads, but wouldn't consider themselves as natural sales people.

After meeting Phil M Jones it took a few months before I accepted that a "business mentor" would probably be a good thing for me, as I can find opportunity in every conversation I have but without focus, and a "sales-funnel" to put them into, I had no vessel to "bottle what I do," so I can stop Doing and start Teaching. So with a huge passion for delivering great results and helping small businesses to grow (or get off the ground), and a determination to make things happen in business, this set me on my way, and now deliver training in a variety of ways and speak professionally for companies and business organisations.

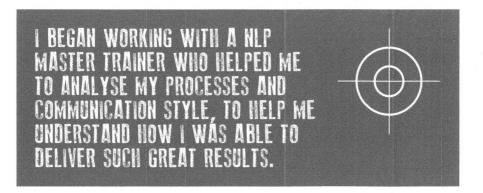

I BEGAN WORKING WITH A NLP MASTER TRAINER WHO HELPED ME TO ANALYSE MY PROCESSES AND COMMUNICATION STYLE, TO HELP ME UNDERSTAND HOW I WAS ABLE TO DELIVER SUCH GREAT RESULTS.

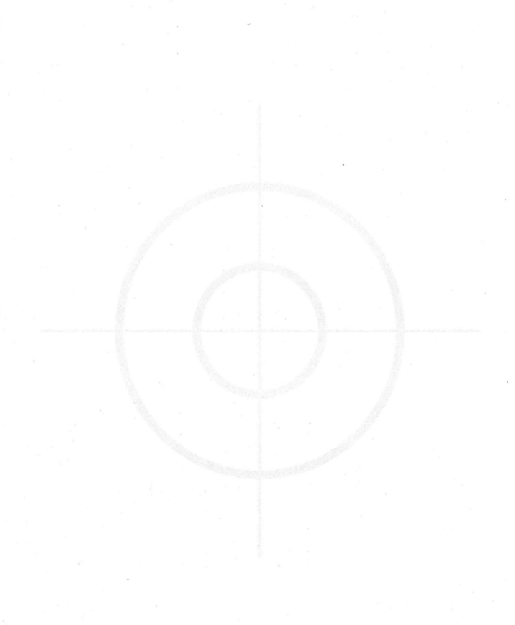

THE GETTING-IN GUIDE

Making business development calls to generate leads is a simple process but must be approached in the right way. To help people that struggle with confidence to pick up the phone or those that aren't very successful on the phone, I often tell them that making business development calls is a bit like ordering pizza!

When I get home hungry and there's nothing in to eat and I can't be bothered to go out, I'll grab a take-way menu from the coffee table drawer, decide what we fancy and after choosing from the menu I pick up the phone and order. I get several pizza menus put through my letter box every month that let me know about the special offers that are available and REMINDING me of their USP (Unique Selling Point), so I don't forget about them – some talk about their authentic pizza base and others talk about using fresh ingredients or making promises to get to you in under 30 minutes. The profile of their target customers is simply, people who might eat pizza (so anyone) and people within their deliver area. They never knock on your door when they're delivering the leaflets to ask if you're hungry now and want to order some pizza... because that's not how it works. Now for you to create something to give to someone to tell them about your business (like a menu), it would cost alot of money to design and produce if it's to do your business justice, and because you probably don't sell a cheap convenience product where people expect to see a flimsy paper menu, you can't just send out thousands of leaflets and expect the phone to ring.

Your phone calls need to be your way of "dropping off a menu", a means of making sure people know who you are and why they might want to do business with you in the future. Don't expect or try to sell on your first call as this is what trips most people up. You spend all day feeling rejected because you're trying to put people under pressure to make a decision that they don't want to make, so the choice is either "yes" or "no". If you take the approach of qualifying them as someone with a potential FUTURE need, then you can put them on into your pipeline and it's just a matter of timing before they will make the decision to buy from you or not. Your aim is to get on their radar and start building a relationship allowing you to gather information about their current solutions (pros & cons), and what is coming up in their business. Conversations that help them to solve little problems will often put you in a position as a "trusted advisor" and someone to go to for help in your specific niche. Helping people to buy is much more enjoyable for both parties rather than one trying to sell to the other. Account managers make the best sales people as they "sit on the client's side of the table" and help them to buy. If you're patient you can begin to instil value and efforts can be made to create urgency, while patiently waiting for them to come to you for help.

Keeping it in context but going to the other end of the scale, if you decide to go out to eat and really wanted to treat yourself, you may try to book a table and you will almost certainly make the effort to dress appropriately. We tend to do this because if the restaurant is up market and the staff are smart we want to make sure we fit in (well, not stand out for the wrong reasons), and don't want to feel uncomfortable or out of place.

If you can apply both these principles to making calls (dropping off a menu and presenting yourself appropriately), you can do what I do and get the attention of anyone you want to work with. By approaching your calls as if you're dropping off your menu with the right finesse it deserves, you won't be perceived as a salesperson, but will come across as a pro-active expert that they were lucky to get chatting with.

The only catch to my approach is that you need to be good at what you do. If you haven't got a proven track record or you're not prepared to put your money where your mouth is, and do a small freebie for potential clients to demonstrate why they might want to do business with you in the future, this method is not for you.

IF YOU HAVEN'T GOT A PROVEN TRACK RECORD OR YOU'RE NOT PREPARED TO PUT YOUR MONEY WHERE YOUR MOUTH IS IT'S HARD TO GET SOMEONE TO CHANGE TO USING YOU

WHAT DO YOU DO?

Ok, so let's start at the beginning with the fundamentals, what do you do? If you offer a variety of products or services, identify what makes the most money and what you enjoy doing the most. If they're not the same thing you need to ask yourself if you want a life style business or if you want to make lots of money?

Now we all like convenience, but a one-stop-shop can give the impression of a "jack of all trades, master of none", so make sure you don't fall into that trap. You need to establish an area of the market or a sector or industry that you've got a proven track record in. THIS IS IMPORTANT because you're going to need this later as part of your pitch.

Don't worry if you're a NEW START-UP, as long as you have experience in a particular niche/sector this is enough to get an opportunity to prove yourself to a potential client, although this often relies on a small freebie or gesture to demonstrate your ability.

We can now start to look at how you're currently branding yourself by looking at your website, any marketing literatures (brochures, price lists, presentation material), on-line marketing activity (advertising, social media, blogging) and how it all looks together. Do you have a well developed image or is your messaging and focus a mish-mash of half-hearted attempts at "marketing"? You don't have to spend loads of money but creating a brand that stands for something is key if you want to establish yourself as the go-to person for a particular product or service in a particular market.

Social media for you and social media for your business are two different things. Your objective of social media for your business should be to establish an on-line presence, allowing search engines like Google to find you quicker and know what you're about (thus helping you to get found when someone is looking for your products or services). It enables you to build a professional picture of you and your business. It's not a good idea to waste time telling people nonsense or getting side tracked with irrelevant long winded posts about what other people are up to on your business page. Also, seeing you tagged in pictures falling out of the pub drunk on Friday night is not a good look professionally, and the old adage, you never get a second chance to make a first impression cannot be stressed enough here.

Just because social media is free it doesn't mean you have to do it all and although I can see the value in some platforms depending on what you are offering, I believe that over 95% is just white noise, and overkill is always a danger. I also believe that nothing comes close to a proper conversation. Social media is a great bolt on, but should not be the be all and end all of any marketing or branding campaign. Remember; people buy people, not Facebook pages, (but more on this later).

This might all sound a bit fluffy but prospecting for new business and trying to convince people to do business with you in the future (when they're not even looking), is much different from dealing with incoming enquiries. By being a proactive expert exploring the market place you can avoid coming across like another salesman on the phone.

SOCIAL MEDIA IS A GREAT BOLT ON, BUT SHOULD NOT BE THE BE ALL AND END ALL OF ANY MARKETING OR BRANDING CAMPAIGN. REMEMBER; PEOPLE BUY PEOPLE, NOT FACEBOOK PAGES

Here are some questions you now need to ask:

- How should you be presenting yourself?

- Looking at your competition, what websites and literature do you like?

- What are your clients looking for and what would they expect to see from someone like you?

WEBSITE

Does your website look professional and is it up to date? Here are a few things you should look at.

Is it clear what you actually do? You have just a few seconds when someone lands on your website while they make their mind up about whether they're in the right place. If what you do is quite technical think about the language you use and remember your site is written for the visitor, many of whom may not want or need to know about the ins and outs of what you do, so try layering the site so people can get to more in-depth information should they wish, without having to sift through loads of text where anything that causes confusion or concern is likely to make people "bounce" and visit someone else's site instead.

Is it clear where people need to go next? People need to be able to navigate through your site to find the information they want. Your Landing pages should be designed specifically to capture the audience of your marketing campaigns, and should aim to get people off that page and actually IN to your site. Stats show that people are much more likely to have a proper look around and explore your site once they've got off your "landing" page.

Is the news/blog section fresh? Latest news articles that are months or years old may make you look like you're not trading anymore, or give the impression you can't be bothered to keep it up to date, or worse, that you have nothing interesting to say! Don't give people an opportunity to question your credibility before you've even got started. When engaged in a longer conversation with someone on the phone, you will often hear people typing and checking you out and when this happens it's great to ask if they're in front of their PC and pointing them to a specific part of your website, or a blog or article.

Are there case studies that demonstrate your expertise? People like to hear stories and see evidence rather than hearing another pitch, so make sure the stories you're telling are relevant to the audience you're trying to attract and approach.

Are you tracking and monitoring your website? If not, why not? There's lots of free analytic tools out there that involve just copying and pasting a line of code into your site. There's plenty of video "how to" guides on YouTube if you use a CMS to update your site yourself (or your web designer will do it for you in a couple of minutes).

I am no analytics expert but there are some obvious things it will tell you if you take a proper look. For example, a print company I was helping had a website for ages before they put in Google analytics and could begin looking at what was going on. After 2 weeks of letting it build up some data about the visitors to the website, we sat down and began to look at what was happening. Straight away we noticed that the contact page had an average page view of less than 3 seconds and was one of the top exiting pages! I know, this wasn't a good sign, so we looked at the page and I made one small suggestion. Because I often go to a contact page to find a number or address, I found that hitting an "enquiry form" to fill out straight away was perhaps putting people off, so we added a short paragraph just about it saying "we'd love to speak with you so please give us a call on 01628 ...... however if you're in a rush or browsing out of hours please feel free to email info@..... Or fill out the form below". Within days we could see that the average page view time on the page had jumped to 17 seconds.

Is your website linked to your social media accounts and other organisations in your sector? You need to create your own web to catch people and funnel them to your website. The search engines like this too!

SOCIAL MEDIA

Social media for business was adopted when people realised that it was free, (well a lot of it is), and it was a great way to boost your search engine rankings (i.e. get you higher in the list) by effectively "piggy-backing" off the back of the larger websites like Facebook. Again, please don't use it to tell people what you're having for lunch or about anything that doesn't continue the continuity of your brand and the professional image you're trying to create.

Facebook certainly has its merits and is a great way to get to consumers, although for a lot of companies working in the business to business arena it can often prove a real distraction and zap up a lot of time posting and blogging with no real rewards, as the audience isn't in a professional/work frame of mind and is there in a "social capacity".

LinkedIn is what I would consider to be the "Facebook" for business. It allows you to create a profile (for you and your company), and is a fantastic way of connecting with your professional contacts. LinkedIn started as a place to create a professional profile/on-line CV, but rather than going down the recruitment route they turned it into a professional social media platform.

There are people out there that now have a full time career teaching people how the use LinkedIn, but the principles and benefits of using it are as follows:

Create the profile you'd like your dream customer to see when they stumble across your details.

Add a professional headshot as people like to see the face that goes with the profile and if you do anything visual then use photos images to make pages look more interesting.

Use your connections to connect you to other people.

When you research your ideal client on LinkedIn not only can you find out who works for the company, but you can often identify the right person you would need to speak to. If they are connected to one of your connections it will show up (usually on the right hand side or when you hover over the little "2nd", next to their name). As long as you have a compelling reason to get in touch with them, then your existing contact will normally put you in touch and will often "warm them up" for you, if you ask nicely. I'll go in to this in more detail later in the book, but you can also find a whole host of useful information about people's career history, which in turn allows you to build up a picture of WHO that person is, and you can start tailoring your approach based on some educated assumptions about what they might respond best to and what might float their boat.

A brief example of how this information can be useful is when I am doing work for IT companies, despite targeting the most senior person I can find, I often need to speak with the IT directors/managers and knowing about their career history gives me an idea of how technical they are and where their expertise lies. If they are more technical than me I will bow to their knowledge, (flattery really does work wonders) and vice versa. I don't want to intimidate someone who's not technical by being blasé with terminology they don't understand.

Many people dabble in social media because it's free and they know they should do something but please remember that your time is valuable, so don't waste it starting groups that no-one wants to join or fishing for leads . If you spend more than a couple of hours per week doing social media for your business, then I would urge you to use that time to pick up the phone and actually speak with potential clients, as it's the most effective way (cost and time wise) to make something happen TODAY. If you want to see results then be proactive and engage with people. Sorry, rant over! I hear too many people complaining about how hard it is out there, to find out they waste many hours every week working harder, not smarter.

Your time is precious, don't waste it!

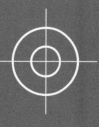

IF YOU WANT TO SEE RESULTS THEN BE PROACTIVE AND ENGAGE WITH PEOPLE. I HEAR TOO MANY PEOPLE COMPLAINING ABOUT HOW HARD IT IS OUT THERE, TO FIND OUT THEY WASTE MANY HOURS EVERY WEEK WORKING HARD, NOT SMART.

WHAT'S STOPPING YOU?

Now it's good to establish what's stopping you before we go any further. I hear all kinds of reasons (excuses!) about why people can't or don't make enough calls, some putting it down to a bad experience and others to a lack of confidence.

To me the "confidence" one can go a little deeper as some people simply don't know how to start a conversation off without coming across like they're trying to sell. Now mix that with the thoughts of "not wanting to interrupt someone's day" or thinking that people won't want to talk to you, and before you've even started you're a nervous bumbling wreck.

For many of us it's hard to blow our own trumpet and we often don't want to come across as cocky, arrogant or be too "salesy", but if you run your own business you can't just rely on someone else to do it for you. This is where I often start with a new client and we look at some of their success stories/case studies and identify who might be interested to know about it. This is where the catch comes in because if you've not got a good track record (i.e. some success stories) then you will find yourself having to do small "freebies" as a way of gaining credibility and building the confidence of a potential client. Some of us claim there isn't enough time to make calls and others I meet simply aren't very proud of their literature/website, which they know is likely to be requested by prospects when you first make contact.

For those that work in an open plan office and particularly in ones that tend to be quiet, the thought of people listening in and hearing you get rejected, or saying something stupid can make the thought of making calls even worse. On the other side of the scale you have those that work in a very busy noisy environment's where it's hard to concentrate with so many distractions going on.

There are also those that don't mind making a few calls but quickly get frustrated with gatekeepers and find themselves getting blocked before they've even had chance to speak to the right person.

Whatever it is that stopping you it probably falls in to 3 main categories - Time, Environment and Beliefs. However please remember that you can manage your time, you can control your environment, and as you read on you'll believe and see that my approach to making "cold calls" is not only an enjoyable process but it generates great results.

PROFILING

M ost companies I meet don't actually know what their USP is, as they don't really do anything different from their competitors. In 99% of cases the only thing that makes your company different is YOU and it's your past experience and the level of service you can deliver that sets you aside.

People buy people, and that's why YOU are the best USP you can use.

I often describe a USP as the companies "personality" so I always start by looking at the people within the business and their expertise and experience. It's best to concentrate on what you're good at as many people starting out in business will take whatever work they can get. This will turn you into a jack of all trades and you will be perceived as a master of none. Doing just the bit you're good at allows you to own your niche and approach new clients as a proactive expert rather than a typical salesman playing a numbers game.

Ok, sales will always be a numbers game but why use a scattergun when you can use a sniper?"

No one really likes to be pitched at, but from a young age we all learn to love stories, so rather than trying to make yourself sound good by using lots of marketing talk (or pitching), you're best off telling a story that's relevant to the person or company you are trying to do business with. This allows you to demonstrate the value of what you do, but without being perceived as a desperate or aggressive salesperson. If you're struggling to think of the right stories to tell, then start by writing some case studies of your best clients. Two similar stories show's a pattern and is compelling evidence that you can do it again. You need to know these stories well as they're NOT to read to someone, just something to refer to as examples.

3 Types of People to Call

If you want to find new customers there are 3 different approaches you can take:

Potential clients - these are companies that are similar to the companies you've helped before. Look at your top 5 clients and identify what they have in common. The more specific you can be, the more compelling your story is and it's this that gives your campaign poise.

Although you may be able to deal with anyone I bet there are some customers that are better than others (spending more, less hassle, negotiations etc), so concentrate on your wish list of clients, ones that help your business to grow in the direction you want. We may like the convenience of a one-stop-shop but most people would rather deal with a specialist especially if the cost is similar.

Only YOU have the ability to deliver a service above and beyond their expectations.

Strategic Partnerships – these are with companies where your products or services complement each other as opposed to being in direct competition with them. "You can sell to my customers and I can sell to yours".

There are likely to be a couple of different strategic partners you could target and if you're struggling to identify them, start by looking at your suppliers or think about other companies that may have approached you in the past.

Some examples might include:

IT support companies can often build strong relationships with their vendors and suppliers and might explore how a pro-active approach, offering to promote someone else's software application to your existing customers is likely to pull in a few extra sales. In return the software house may be able to outsource some of their customer support to your company or pass referrals across!

For a printer it's often worth working closely with local design companies as you can help bring their designs to life, helping them win over more clients. The other benefit of this relationship is that artwork is much more likely to be in the correct format/ quality and people spending money on design often have a budget for printing too.

For products and services that are more project based (i.e. interior design, removals, cabling/IT hardware companies), you need to think about other services people will be searching for, like building surveyors and commercial estate agents as these are likely to get engaged by a potential client before they start thinking about designs, removals etc. These are people that are likely to come into contact with your potential clients, and what YOU do is something that they might get asked from time to time.

A great way to start the ball rolling is to offer up an opportunity for them to explore. This could be one of your customers or contacts that has asked you about something that you can't or don't offer, or you've pointed out the importance of this product or service as part of the project you're delivering for them. You don't give presents to receive, but referrals seem to work in that way. If you give someone two referrals or opportunities to explore you'll often find them asking "what can I do for you in return?" If you're sticking to what you do best, not trying to do anything and everything in your field, you'll find that you will build great relationships with those around you that are best at what they do and they will see you as the expert at what you do.

Introducers - this is your referral network, people you meet that like you and what you do as a business (e.g. your ethos, approach), it could be someone you've met networking or people you're connected with on LinkedIn. It's crucial that you stay in touch with these people but you need to get the balance right. Calling them weekly to ask if they've come across anyone looking for *xyz* will only start to annoy them so make sure they understand exactly what you're looking for and who you can help, as this will help them to identify the right people to recommend you contact, or point in your direction. A monthly catch up call to find out what they've been up to and telling them a quick success story of yours will make sure they remember you and often your story will trigger a memory of someone they hadn't previously thought of that they could connect you with.

Asking your introducers to warm people up for you, or simply being able to use their name will often stop you feeling like you're about to "cold call" someone, and if what you do really is relevant then they won't mind, although sometimes discretion is required if you're getting "inside information".

If you find yourself on LinkedIn researching someone you want to contact (then firstly, well done you, it's one of the most useful resources for professional profiling), then look at any 2nd level connections that they may be able to introduce you to. My 350 contacts connect me with 6.9 million professionals!!!

Preparing and Perfecting your Pitch

Pitching to someone that has approached you is totally different from the pitch you will use on the phone when prospecting for new business. Because so many people believe that pitching is all about making a sale there and then, it means that us patient professionals out there, can build trust, respect and rapport with people, as many of us prefer someone who wants to help us make a decision, than someone that is just trying to sell to us. A great quote from the best sales trainer I've ever met is this:

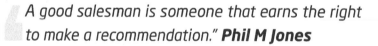 *A good salesman is someone that earns the right to make a recommendation."* **Phil M Jones**

So rather than trying to think of a fancy set of words, I always look at a pitch as telling a story. As children we were inherently engaged by stories and we quickly got taken on an emotional rollercoaster where our imagination ran away with us and it's something that stays with most of us for life (hence why the film industry is worth so much).

Your stories should effectively be case studies and the moral of the story needs to highlight the VALUE of the part YOU played in it. Not all about you, or even about the product or service itself, but of the outcomes, results and benefits to the person or company in a "big picture" way. If you have a testimonial from the clients you're talking about it adds credibility to your story and can be used as a reason for the call, to share your good news/achievement with someone that might be interested.

Blowing your own trumpet is hard for most of us as we don't want to be seen as arrogant and often where most sales people go wrong is when their confidence is received as being smarmy, cocky or condescending. If you wouldn't consider yourself to be a natural salesperson then you'll probably find that you're going to be better than you think because most of us put up a barrier when we think people are trying to sell to us. If people don't perceive you as a typical salesperson they're far more likely to be open and honest with you, which puts you in a position where you can ask the important questions, which in turn leads to a decision being made.

For many consultants the story is more about them as individuals, telling people about your past successes and linking how they all build up to position YOU as the "go-to" person in your particular niche or sector. This allows you to build your credibility and gives your story a path to follow, which should end with why you think they are going to want to do business with you in the future.

REMEMBER – Prospecting over the phone is like dropping off a pizza menu. Remember what I said before - they don't knock on your door asking if you're hungry now, they simply remind you of their USP and special offers to keep it fresh in your mind (so you don't forget about them).

Making a decision to buy is often more about timing than anything else, so when you're prospecting over the phone, your initial conversation is your opportunity to QUALIFY a prospect of having a potential future need, before they can go into to your pipeline.

Typically "sales" is all about closing, whereas prospecting (making business development calls), is about generating leads and establishing future opportunities. People want to feel they can make a decision in their own time and if you push for a sale and force a decision there and then, while you're on the phone, the likelihood is that you'll just get lots of no thank yous, as it's probably not something that's on the top of their priority list!

TYPICALLY "SALES" IS ALL ABOUT CLOSING, WHEREAS PROSPECTING (MAKING BUSINESS DEVELOPMENT CALLS), IS ABOUT GENERATING LEADS AND ESTABLISHING FUTURE OPPORTUNITIES.

RESEARCHING YOUR PROSPECTS

When you're working from a wish list of potential clients (as opposed to a huge database), it's far less daunting and knowing that just one of these becoming a client could make all the difference to your business, often helps give you the focus and direction that's needed to make this happen.

The more you can find out about your prospects before you call the easier it is to control and positively influence your conversations. By taking a proper look at someone's website, LinkedIn profile, blogs and social media, you can then start building a picture of who it is you will be contacting.

And when I say "who" you will be contacting, I don't just mean their name. There are plenty of places to access information on-line and the more information you can gather about a person the clearer the picture you can paint.

> As I said before, a *good example of this is when I am promoting IT services to potential customers. It's VERY useful to know if someone has a technical background. If I can see they've work as an engineer or consultant then I know to bow to their technical knowledge (flattery works wonders), and I won't allow myself to get tripped up if they throw a curve ball, as just one example you don't know what you're talking about is enough to wipe out any credibility you've managed to build. Likewise if I'm targeting an IT director and I can see that they were a finance director in their past role, I will use my story to highlight the value of a product or service to their business as opposed to the details of what the product or service is.*

People often don't lock down their social media profiles so you may find that you can see people's latest pictures and comments, which can help you to make some educated assumptions about what might float their boat. If you can see someone has lots of pictures of their dogs or cats, then there is a fair assumption to be made that the subject of pets is likely to be something that will get them talking. Other examples I've used may be when I can see someone is collecting sponsorship for a marathon, so being direct and asking about how their training is going might be an easy way to get them talking and feeling at ease with you.

If you can't find anything on-line about the person you should be contacting then a quick call to your prospects receptionist to say, "I wanted to send some information about *xyz* and I was wondering who I should address it to?" will often get you a name, and it is a prime opportunity to ask some questions about when is likely to be the best time to follow it up, and how.

Sometimes the smallest of details will help to get someone talking so if a receptionist tells you, "they've had to leave early to take their dog to the vet" or "they're away doing an exhibition but will be back next week", then I would use this as an ice-breaker when I call back.

I might say something like, "Hi John, I've been trying to get hold of you for a while now but before I tell you what it's all about I am curious to know how the exhibition went last week? I thought I would leave it a few days as I imagine you're still playing catch-up?" and then let them talk.

So, what does your research tell you about your prospects, and is what people find about YOU giving them the right message?

PREPARING TO MAKE CALLS

Getting in the right frame of mind is crucial as your attitude comes across in your voice and that often says more than the words you use. A study shows that less than 10% of what we're saying as humans is coming out of our mouths, as 90% is body language, gestures and facial expressions. This means that we only have 10% of our communication ability over the phone, and with 7% of this being down to pitch, pace, volume and tone, it is often less important which words you choose and more about how they are delivered.

Smile while you dial may be cheesy, but it really helps as your mood will come across in your voice. Smiling causes your body to release chemicals which make us feel good, so I often start my day by finding a fun joke or video and here (to your left) is a picture of my "smile wall". These are photos from my travels and loved ones and I can't help but smile when I look at them. Having them right in front of you makes them hard to ignore.

No-one wants to feel like a cold caller so by taking the time to profile exactly who you will be targeting (making sure you're playing to the strengths of the business), and using the call to "get on their radar", you will NOT be perceived as a cold caller, but be seen as a Pro-Active Expert. Many people will thank you for calling, and having them knowing and believing that they are lucky you have stumbled across their details and bothered to pick up the phone is essential to motivate yourself to start making those calls.

As I've mentioned earlier, sales will always be a numbers game but your phone allows you to be a sniper. That old chestnut saying "each NO is one step closer to your next YES" is rubbish!! If you get two NO's on the trot, you're either calling the wrong people or using the wrong approach.

Get comfortable in your working environment. Many of us find ourselves working in open plan offices and that feeling of people listening in, hearing you getting rejected or not wanting to sound stupid can make you feel flustered or embarrassed, particularly in a quiet office. You need to be "in the zone" when you're on the phone with people, so limiting visual distractions can help. Try facing away from others or finding a quiet corner to work in. Background noise or a quiet radio can be a great way to create atmosphere and stop you feeling like you're being listened to. When I get to work from home I use a radio for a couple of reasons:

It doesn't sound like I'm in a quiet room all by myself and it makes me tap my feet! I like a little sing-along to the radio in car in the morning as it's a great way to wake me up and warm up my voice.

Music can be really powerful and nostalgic, it changes our mood and creates an atmosphere. That feeling when you find yourself tapping your feet without thinking or singing along to your favourite song at the top of your voice can elevate your mood instantly. For me "it's a beautiful day" by U2 is a great one to start your day with, but I did work with someone who used the Rocky theme tune in the car to "pump themselves up" just before a meeting! It is down to personal preference, although I wouldn't recommend having thrash metal or gangster rap blaring away in the back ground!

Having a small "wish list" means you don't have to make lots of calls and for many clients I worked for over a long period I would look to have 1 or 2 positive conversations in each session, breaking it down into 1-2 hour chunks. I would often reward myself with some fresh air (a cigarette break and a cup of tea), but when dealing with a sales team you need to know what motivates them and what would be seen as a worthy reward. Sometimes simply offering a small cash incentive for the person with the most appointments can work, but when commission is being paid anyway or it's starting to cost you a small fortune, then early finishes and late starts can help motivate some people more. A group reward for a team might be buying them all pizza for lunch if they hit an agreed target by lunchtime. It's hard to know what will work best but you'll often find money isn't always the best motivator for some people.

GETTING PAST THE GATEKEEPER

This is a common hurdle that many of us struggle with and it can get rather frustrating when you don't even get a chance to speak with the decision maker and explain to them exactly why you're calling.

Being told by a receptionist "just send something to info@abc.... and someone will come back to you if they're interested!" doesn't help, as you know it probably won't get to the right person and even if it does, are they likely to read something from someone they've never heard of or spoken to before?

Here are some pointers to help you get past the gatekeeper, with tips and techniques I use on a day to day basis, depending on what mood I'm in and who I am calling:

Asking for someone by name will always help although it doesn't mean you won't get asked what the call is about. By saying "Hi there, can I speak with John please? (brief pause) sorry, John Smith", in a bubbly or over-familiar voice you can give the impression that you already know him. This will reduce the number of times you're asked "what is the call about?"

Use the gatekeeper to gather information. If you're really nice to them they will often help you but you must be careful not to come across as a "sales person". Often it's the confident sounding sales people that will get blocked as they sound too bubbly and happy that the person answering the phone immediately thinks "it's a sales call", and the barrier will come up. Using a shy/nervous/bumbling voice with a flustered start, saying something like "Oh...um....I wondered if you can help me?" PAUSE! As human's we like to help others and most people can't help but say "Yes" or "I'll try" when asked that question. You can then say "it's a bit of an 'off the cuff' call really, but I work for a company called ABC Ltd and I've been asked to introduce myself to [the person] there that looks after IT, and I was wondering what's the best way to go about it?" To this you will often be told that in the first instance you're best off sending an email, to which I always reply saying "that's not a problem although I don't normally like sending emails unless I've spoken with people first, and I'm not sure what I will send until I've spoken with him, so is there a good time to call back when I'm likely to catch him?"

If you can't find a name online then use your first call just to find it out. By saying "Hi there, I've been ask to send in some information about xyz and I want to confirm your address is.. (read it from their website)..." they will say "yes, that's correct" and then you say "great, and who should I be sending to?", prompting them to tell you.

Leave a message, don't leave a message? I try not to leave message as part of my "avoiding rejection" (covered in more detail later in this book), as it often leaves the ball in their court and after leaving 10 messages and no-one returning your call, you can feel deflated and like no-one wants to talk to you. Leave a second message and it begins to feel like you're chasing them and often increases their reluctance to take your call. If you're forced to leave a message I would always keep it brief, trying to create intrigue as opposed to telling them what I want, maybe saying something like, "hi John, my name is Anthony Stears and I work for ABC Ltd and one of our directors has asked me to get in touch with you. If you get a couple of minutes please give me a call back, I'm in and out of meetings over the next couple of days so if I we don't speak by Friday, I will give you a call when I'm back in the office. My number is 07.......and again it is Anthony". This approach is more likely to get a response than saying I want to talk to you about our offering of xyz and is a good way of keeping control of the prospect and taking final responsibility for the next action (step 5 of the call structure).

Being politely persistent is the key. A professional manner and saying things like "it's not urgent so at the risk of playing telephone tennis perhaps I will call again when I'm back in the office/have a gap between meetings" tells the gatekeeper that you're a busy person too (much like the person you're trying to get hold of), and this can often be a good way of suggesting that you don't have time to answer their questions. If you use the same approach on the same person they will start to remember you and once you have their name you can use it, being really friendly and politely asking "Hi Jane, It's only Anthony here, I don't suppose John is free for a couple of minutes is he?".

After a while they will remember who you are and you can then get them to tell you when is a good time to try again. They often feel slightly bad if the person isn't available when you call, and once they feel like they've let you down and have appreciated your patient nature they will do their best to help.

Some cheeky little tricks

Whenever I get asked "what my call is about" I will usually give 1 of 2 answers:

Either "Oh... don't worry it's not urgent, is there a better time when I could call back?" to which they will often say "hold on a minute, let me just try their line" or "actually, if you call back after 3pm you've more likely to catch them".

Or, I will say "Yes, sorry, I've been asked to get in touch but if now isn't a good time, perhaps I should call back. Can you suggest a time I'm likely to catch them?". If you get through using this technique and they question you on your statement of "being asked to get in touch", I am always ready to say "I'm sorry if your receptionist got the wrong impression but it was my director that has asked me to get in touch as he's keen to introduce himself to YOU because......(into pitch/story).

In the second situation above I will often use a "cut-off" technique. Before they have finished their reply to answer my question (and before they get chance to ask me one), I say "That's great! Thanks Jane", this suggests I have finished with the conversation and gives me a good chance they will try the persons line without asking me any questions.

Saying you are returning someone's call is cheeky and there is a good chance you will get pulled up on it, however if you have left this person a recent voice mail then there is a way out of it. If the person you get put through to answers by saying "I didn't leave you a message" be ready to use the line "I'm sorry John, I was passed a message from the office just saying "John returned my call, and there were no other details so I assumed it was you! Obviously it wasn't, but seeing as I've got you on the phone I was hoping to speak with you because ....blah blah blah". You will need confidence to pull this one off and it's not for the faint hearted.

A dismissive or derogatory tone of voice can stop you getting asked too many questions and I will often find myself using this when I am approaching someone that is a doctor or very senior in a big organisation. By using a posh voice and asking politely in a slightly rushed manner, you treat the receptionist's like their questions are a formality you don't have time for.

Saying something like "can I speak with John please...sorry, I mean Dr John Smith?". Their first question will always be "and who can I say is calling?", to which I say my FULL name, making huge emphasis on the pronunciation of my surname, like that is the import detail and all I feel she needs to put me through! If another question is asked about what the call is regarding I revert back to the "oh, it's not urgent, if now isn't a good time perhaps I should call back?", then shut up. They will very rarely repeat the question and will either try to put you through or suggest a time to call back.

If flattery, charm and the little tricks don't work you can always go down the bribery route. Sending in a small gift (a branded freebie perhaps/something useful or a box of cakes), will often go down well and if there's a compliment slip or business card inside you have a good reason to follow them up to check they were received and they enjoyed them. Getting a positive association with your name and business can really help and I've used individual cupcakes to PA's many a time to get them on side and have suggested that we will bring a box when we come for our meeting. This works on a couple of levels as it's very presumptive, which can subliminally convinces them that is the case, and plus who doesn't like cake!!!!

Try to think of gatekeepers as someone that can help you. They usually know who's who, what suppliers they use and can often tell you useful information about the people you need to speak with. Not just things like, when you're likely to catch them but what that person might like or prefer, and often in smaller companies they may even reveal other information about what's in that persons diary or personal details about family/pets/interests etc...

Do remember that this is not telesales or even telemarketing, it's about making business development calls. It's much more of an enjoyable process when you chip away at a wish list of clients, patiently waiting for the right time, rather than playing the numbers game and taking the mentality that each "no" is one step closer to the next "yes". To me this is rubbish as 2 "no's" on the trot means you're either calling the wrong people or taking the wrong approach.

Pitch Perfection.

> DO REMEMBER THAT THIS IS NOT TELESALES OR EVEN TELEMARKETING, IT'S ABOUT MAKING BUSINESS DEVELOPMENT CALLS.

CALL STRUCTURE

I try not to write "call scripts" as people tend to read them (rather than learn them), which is bad for 2 main reasons. Firstly, as children we love to be read to but as adults we tend to find it boring or patronising and it's quite easy to detect if someone is reading off a script. If you think someone is reading down the phone most of us automatically assume it's a sales call and the barriers go up or we switch off.

At this point you should now know the approach you're going to be using and have an impressive story or 2 to tell. Your "pitch" should be a story (your story), that your potential customer can relate too. The pitch you use when you are prospecting is slightly different from the one you would use with inbound enquiries as you're NOT speaking with someone who is ready to buy (or at least they don't think they are).

Where so many of us go wrong with prospecting over the phone is that we try to rush things and many sales people try to get to the point of asking the question of "do you want to buy?" far too soon. If you force a decision before someone is ready to make it, you'll find that most will simply say "no". (This is where the mentality of "each no is one step closer to your next yes" started - and again, this is rubbish)!!

The art of prospecting is to look for FUTURE opportunities so you have time to nurture the prospect and earn the right to make a recommendation. By concentrating on qualifying your prospects as having a potential future need, you can then gage when THEY see themselves making the decision to take action. (You can speed up this process and this is explained in the section "the art of a perfect follow-up"). As you qualify your prospects you can begin to build rapport, trust, respect and you then add them to your pipeline.

I find that if the prospect finds the story compelling enough the call will be a catalyst for them to take action and typically 1 in 5 that gets qualified will be compelled to take action now. This is partly down to the conversational approach (not a sales pitch), and the fact that the story highlights an area of "pain/inefficiency" in their business and the decision they may have thought about (or procrastinated over but never seemed important enough to do anything about), is now seen as an opportunity to improve. "Phew... thank god they were called by a pro-active expert that actually understands their pain and has a proven track record in offering a solution to people/business just like them!!!!"

The Call Structure you need to follow for lead generation and finding opportunities is as follows:

1. **Intro and Teaser**
2. **Establish a potential future need**
3. **"The chat"**
4. **Agreeing the next action**
5. **Taking final responsibility for next contact**

1. Intro and Teaser

Obviously, you must say your name and where you're calling from but this needs to be followed up with a compelling reason as to why YOU phoned THEM.

Example when speaking to a potential client

"Hi there John, sorry to bother you but one of my directors has asked me to get in touch and I'm hoping to chat with you for a minute or two, (slight pause), or perhaps there is a good time to call back?" (If they sound busy or reluctant to speak then back away and schedule a call back).

They'll often find that because you seemed to have backed away you won't be perceived as a sales person and they're likely to say something like, "I've got a couple of minutes now quickly" and I will then continue, "Well, my name is Anthony Stears and I work for a company called ABC limited based over in Reading, not far from you guys (this is first reason - "we're local"). The reason for the call is that we provide IT Support (tell them what we do), and although I imagine you have this all covered at the moment (get the objection out the way and let them know you're not expecting them to buy today), we're trying to be a bit proactive (people like that word) at the moment, and because we've been doing such great stuff for (insert name of past clients - gives credibility and shows a proven track record in their business sector), we're making a bit of a name for ourselves (showing pride - not arrogance). Anyway, my director (making it personal) has come across YOUR details (makes them feel special), and has asked me to get in touch and see if he could come and introduce himself ?" (telling them what we want). Taking a short pause then saying "we're not expecting to sell to you or sign you up, but what I am hoping is that we'll impress you enough, that when you are looking to review your current solution that hopefully you'll remember us and get in touch! So, I was wondering if you could spare maybe half an hour over the next few weeks and I'll get "the boss" to pop over and have a chat with you." ("popping over for a coffee" sounds less formal/salesy than "booking a meeting".

Now this might seem a bit long winded but it's open, honest and doesn't come across like a sale pitch.

Example if you're calling a potential Strategic Partner

"Hi there John/Mr Director, My Name is Anthony Stears and I work for ABC Ltd in Reading, not far from you guys. Please excuse me as this is a bit of a random call really, but one of my directors found your details (or maybe "has been keeping an eye on what you're up to") and has asked me to get in touch. Are you ok to talk for a couple of minutes or is there a good time when I could call back?" (by backing away at such an early point, you will find people are much more receptive to speaking with you, and will hear you out). As above they will often say something like "I've got a couple of minutes now, what's it all about?" and I would go one to say something like "Well, as I mentioned I work for ABC Ltd and do IT support for local SME's and we're getting asked more and more about (insert what they do - "providing hardware" or "your finance/CRM software" as another example), and we're looking for a GOOD local company we can work with that might be able to help some of our clients out. I'm not saying we'll have loads of leads for you every month but it is something that's coming up more often, and we're trying to be pro-active and we're looking to build relationships with reputable suppliers (or I might say "strategic partners") in the local area, and when we came across your details we really wanted to get in touch (bit of flattery). (Short pause) If I'm honest I'm hoping that perhaps we can help some of your clients too as I do some of the sales and marketing stuff here, but at this stage I was wondering if you think it's worth having a coffee with my boss and exploring this opportunity?"

2. Establishing a potential future need

This is crucial and often by using the intro and teasers above this comes automatically as they agree/accept the reasons you have given for getting in touch. You are making an educated assumption by profiling your prospects first, however if you're calling a company that is about to stop trading (for example), they will often pipe-up and tell you at the end of your intro. Although I would ask if any of their existing clients are being passed on to anyone else (because you never know!), I would happily accept that there's not really an opportunity for work in the future and therefore I can decide not to waste too much time, and move on to the next one.

Please note that although we're only looking for future needs, some might be years in the future and others may be months or weeks away. This is relevant and important to know as this will determine how much time and effort goes in to contacting and when that should be.

e.g. if someone tells you they're signed into a support contract till the end of the year, you want to be suggesting that perhaps

October/November time would be good for you to go and see them. It's best to go when THEY are ready to give it the focus it deserves and the only way I would push for or accept a meeting sooner, is if I could identify (and get the prospect to admit) any issues that perhaps is not being fixed or supported by their existing solution.

3. The chat

This is often described as "objection handling" by most sales trainers and is where most pushy sales guys fail on the phone as they brashly try to convince the prospect they want what they offer, by throwing features and benefits at them, in a sales pitch like fashion.

A first call/first contact should not be about trying to sell but simply about awareness, letting the potential client know you are there and giving them a compelling reason as to why they might want to do business with you in the future (which could be tomorrow, or it could be next year). You want to be seen as a pro-active expert and earn the right to make a recommendation (when asked by the client) by building rapport, credibility and trust. You need to be seen as "helping them to buy" and not "trying to sell to them".

To me, this part of the conversation is all about gathering useful information, ammunition if you like, that I can use later to demonstrate I've listened and can justify the recommendation

I will get asked to make. Now, asking probing questions helps reveal some of these answers and I will go into more detail later in the book (in the follow up call section) how you can use your manners to ask almost any question, but be aware that constant questioning will come across more like an interrogation and 2-3 blunt questions on the trot will make it blatantly obvious what you're trying do. The person you're speaking with will start to feel like you're leading them somewhere, and may feel they're not ready or liking where it is going. If they feel like that, it goes back to being a "sales call" and the barriers go up.

You want them to be doing most of the talking however this is the time when you may wish to elaborate on your "story", telling them about the testimonial you received and the reported results your clients have found. Sometimes it's only when you talk about issues, problems and inefficiencies that people similar to them have experienced, that they too will own up to having or will relate to what you are saying. I find it's much more powerful to say what someone's thinking and have them agree or relate to me, and it's a great way establish yourself as the go-to-expert, and someone that actually understands their business/people/ issues/problems etc...

This is how you get perceived as the proactive expert and not a "cold caller", and it's at this point you will find people will actually begin thanking you for making the effort to call them! It's this approach that seems to make me stand out and it's why

I don't like to consider myself a "sales trainer" but someone that shows businesses how to stand out, by offering an excellent personal service and helping their clients to buy, acting more like the "account manager" for a client (that doesn't realise they are going to sign up or buy). You have to know someone, the problems they are having and what's important to them before you're at a position where you can confidently offer a solution.

Please note this part of the conversation may not happen on the first call if the person you're speaking with doesn't have the time to talk properly or could be out and about on their mobile. This doesn't matter and the key to it is that you're the one that brings it to a close and completes the final two steps to the call structure. When someone is opening up and we've been speaking for over 5 or 10 minutes, I love using the line "I feel like I could speak to you for ages" or perhaps something like "there's loads I'd love to ask you, but I don't want to take up too much of your time. I'd love an opportunity to come over and introduce my boss, so could you spare half an hour or so over the next couple of weeks, when we could pop over and introduce ourselves properly?"

Closing every call is the same and it must finish with these two steps.

4.You need to agree the next action

This must be what THEY want or have asked for and it's important this is made clear before the call ends.

5.YOU must take final responsibility of when you will next speak.

It's important to discuss what is going to happen next to conclude the call and move things forward.

Now, this may be that you need to call back because they didn't have long enough to hear your story (only your teaser), so ask them when is going to be good to catch them, when you'll have their undivided attention. Sometimes you'll find that the suggestion of "perhaps early next week" or asking " is there a good day or time of day when I'm likely to catch you? I'm not sure if perhaps early in the morning or at the back of the day would work best?" pause slightly to give them chance to think and respond, and say "I mean, what would work for you?", then SHUT UP. Note if they tell you quickly that Friday (for example) is a good day I would always asked if there' s a good time to call, and I say "I'll put that in my diary and look forward to speaking with you then." (you'll see how this can help when you do your follow up call later in book).

If you find that the person you were speaking with seemed distracted or slightly uninterested and says something like "can you just send some information across please?" I will always say "Yes, no problem," and would continue to confirm their email address. I would then follow that up with "If I'm honest I usually like to have a bit of a chat with people when I send something over, so let me leave it with you and if there's any immediate questions or queries then you've got my details, BUT so I don't forget about it, I'll make a quick note to touch base in a week or 2 just in case it doesn't get through spam filters or you can't find our details." Now sometimes they may say something like "actually I'm about to go on holiday/do an exhibition/finish off a project (whatever it may be), so can we say next month?", this is always okay, as you need to understand that speaking to you is not at the top of their priority list right now and you don't want to push them too hard and force a decision because you know what the answer is likely to be! If however they respond saying something like "I'd rather you didn't." or "nah, just leave it with us and we'll come back to you if we're interested." then you can take that as brush off and your teaser either didn't do the job or you simply caught them having a bad day and I would try my luck again 3-4 weeks later, where if the response to me is the same I would come to the conclusion that they don't have a future need that they can see, or, that they are actually quite rude and not the sort of client we would want anyway, (that's not to say I wouldn't try them again 6-12 months later as people move on and things change).

BUILDING RAPPORT

There are some simple fundamentals to building rapport and being open and honest is always the best approach, but I always start by saying that you need to make people feel special. Because you will have done your research already you may use something like telling someone you're looking at their LinkedIn page, and using that as the reason you called. You might use their career history (displayed on the LinkedIn profile) as the reason for your call, noticing that they are just the sort of people you should be speaking with, etc.....

Flattery really does work and I usually describe the approach as being like "courting" in the old fashioned sense of the word, where you had to work hard to impress a girl before you got what you wanted. As opposed to the modern approach of going for easy, quick, one-night stands with someone who isn't wife material, to say the least!!!! Sorry if this analogy offends anyone but this helps demonstrate that the good old fashioned "English gentlemen" approach has much more integrity than the predator/ sleazy salesman looking for easy prey.

Just in case, the other way I like to look at it is to treat them like I would my father-law (who I respect and am slightly scared of, and wouldn't want to intentionally offend), who is someone I want to think highly of me and that I want to be seen to be making an effort for.

Demonstrating your research/preparation (like using their website, blog or LinkedIn profile), will always help build rapport with someone, so tell them what you've found out about them and their company and why that's of interest to you. It stops them feeling like they are just another person on your list/ database and shows you've taken an interest in them. Remember people's favourite topic is themselves so by talking about them, they will often continue and fill in any gaps or correct any inaccurate information or assumptions you have.

Put your money where your mouth is. This is where "the catch" is with my approach as you need to be ready to supply testimonials, case studies and/or be prepared to offer a small freebie as way of demonstrating how good you are. e.g. as described earlier in the book, with an IT support company I may offer to try and resolve issues that their existing supplier hasn't addressed, using this as a way to convince them to change to me in the future.

You need to be professional yet personable. People buy people and although you are a representation of your company you're NOT a robot reading a script, you are trying to have an intelligent business conversation. If you're a small company and making the calls for yourself (as opposed to one of your sales team), you need to remember that YOU are your USP and it's your history and past successes that are the story (pitch) you should be talking about. As long as you're clear when you are giving your opinion (and not fact) and you justify any comments and recommendations that you make, then you will come across as credible and knowledgeable. If you don't know the answer to something, don't be afraid to say "I don't know" or "I'm not 100% sure?" You can say something like "I think that.......but I will find out for sure and come back to you, if that's ok?" If you're looking to book appointments for your boss or someone else, this is a prime time to say "It's actually my boss (then give their full name) who is the expert on this stuff, so perhaps we could arrange for him to pop over and introduce himself and he should be able to answer all your questions." I then quickly follow it up with "I'll see if I can come along too as it would be nice to put a face to the name, and I've really enjoyed chatting with you", then

SHUT UP. This last bit of flattery usually makes them feel more comfortable to accept the meeting and keeps it personal.

In a meeting situation, as long as you take the approach of going there to introduce yourself and find out more about them, you can patiently demonstrate your reluctance to sell at them, and you can then turn your "sales pitch" into stories about clients that have had similar problems to the ones they have revealed and go on to tell them how YOU managed to resolve them. Only at that point can you confidently offer to do the same for them and suggest steps they could take to move forwards. Sometimes baby steps are better and although it takes longer before the client starts spending big money with you, you're VERY unlikely to upset them by asking for too much and you'll often find that when you are "prospecting", you have to deal with the 'scraps' of work on offer to demonstrate why YOU are so good. You then earn the right of being a "trusted adviser and expert" and will get the opportunity to consult with them further and find other areas you might be able to help.

Building rapport on the phone is important and there are many different ways you can achieve this, but the cardinal rule is not just to listen but to actually pay attention. Another reason I don't write scripts is because if you're paying attention to the conversation you will know what to say next and no script can pre-empt exactly what someone will say to you first. Reading a script will distract you from listening and actually paying attention.

The next exercise is what I believe enables me to keep people talking for longer periods of time and get them to open up to me, quickly building rapport.

Reading between the lines and the power of implication -

When you're looking at someone, scientists have shown that only 10% of what we are saying is actually coming out of our mouths. Most of what we say is in our body language, gestures and facial expressions. This means that when we're on the phone we only have 10% of our communication ability!

Then, when you then look at the remaining 10% of what we're trying to say, 7% of that is actually in our tone, pitch and pace, highlighting that the words we choose are less important than how they are delivered.

One of my favourite exercises demonstrates the power of a conversation and makes many people sit up and think about what messages are being received from their marketing campaigns when clients have nothing but the written word. So here goes, what does this sentence mean?

"I didn't say he stole the money"

Without any tone it means exactly what the words say, but how many meanings can this simple sentence have without changing any of the words, or the order of them?

Putting emphasis on just one word, any word, changes the meaning of the sentence. Emphasising the "I" implies that someone else has said "he stole the money". On the "didn't" it shows a strong/ adamant denial that you said "he stole the money". And so on.....

So that means that this simple sentence could now have 8 different meanings before we look at throwing sarcasm, intrigue or concern into the mix. Now there are a couple of reasons why I go into this as part of my training, as you can use it to imply things, allowing you to suggest that their current solution isn't giving them everything they need and deserve, without looking unprofessional and trying to slate or bad-mouth your competition. This can allow you to rub salt in the wound (so to speak), and talk about a weakness, issue or area of their business, without it coming across rude, condescending or patronising. It allows you to "plant a seed" of a solution without trying to sell to them, letting them find the answer by themselves.

The other reason this exercise is important, is it can increase your awareness and gives you the ability to read between the lines when people are talking TO YOU, and it is in the way you react to what they say that will keep their attention and make you stand out. Simple examples maybe when you can hear in someone's voice that they are rushed or in a busy, noisy environment, and this is where I would instantly say "you sound rather busy" or "you don't sound like you're having a great day" or perhaps "it sounds like you're out and about at the moment, is there a good time I might catch you either later this afternoon or over the next few days?" This will usually do one of two things. If they are really busy they might say something like "yeah, that would be great, I'm flat out at the moment," and they will often go on to suggest a good day or time to call back (appreciative that you have respected their time). Or, what sometimes happens, particularly if there is a slight undertone of being pissed off, tired, rushed, deflated etc,is the realisation that perhaps they came across as being a bit rude, at which point most of us will apologise (perhaps justifying our tone by revealing something like "they just had a supplier let them down", or someone in the office has upset them).

If someone starts off rude or hostile towards you the best thing to do is back away. Having said that, I would do it in a way that lets them know I have sensed their hostility, and would put it down to them having a bad day and not a personal thing towards me, simply bad timing! Being extra polite in these situations makes it very hard for someone to continue being rude or harsh towards you and if they continue, I would ask myself if they're actually someone I would like to deal with as a customer.

Manners are a tool, they enable you to defuse heated situations, ask nearly any question you want and they can be used to help you avoid rejection (explained more in the "motivating yourself to make calls" chapter). Manners don't cost a thing and if you combine them with the phrase "if you don't ask, you don't get" you'll be surprised at what people will say yes to if you ask the right question or ask for the right thing to happen next.

Taking lots of notes when you're speaking with someone and typing or writing them ALL up when you've finished, is crucial. Scribbling down things that they say means you won't forget to address or respond and you can quote their words later on and use that as the reason for telling them a particular "story". I can use their words back at them in a mirroring effect, but sometimes this can seem like your trying to twist their word, so quoting them to clarify understanding tends to work best. You can also quote them as a questioning technique asking them to explain what they meant by xyz, or clarifying your understanding of what they said, saying something "so is that a bit like ......?"

Another reason you need to make lots of notes is that you can't remember every detail from every conversation you have. It is the little details that are your ammunition, so make sure you write as much as you can after the call, as all of this can be used to jog their memory later on and is a great demonstration that you're the sort of person that pays attention to detail (people like that, particularly in the context of business).

Prospect management is key to staying on top of your pipeline, not letting anything slip through the net, and storing this information is VERY important. This is why I have dedicated a small section of this book to explain the importance of using a CRM's (Customer Relationship Management Systems), in one form or another.

A good CRM system is one you (or your staff), know how to use. It's a place where you can store lots of information (contact details, research, notes, etc), and it should have the ability to remind you to do things, like when to follow someone up. Now, some systems allow you to analyse the contacts and run "filters" so you can identify key prospects for specific marketing campaigns, but this is only something you tend to do when you've had chance to populate it and have created some activity to analyse or monitor, so don't get to hung up on this or use any excuses to delay the transition to using a CRM system.

To keep it simple I have **3** effective CRM systems you can use to manage your prospects FOR FREE and I've highlighted the Pros & Cons of each.

The 1-31 system – It's a paper based system of "drop-files" that sit in a filing cabinet somewhere. This can be great for those that don't like using computers and can be very useful to the "network marketers" who collect lots of business cards as they move from event to event.

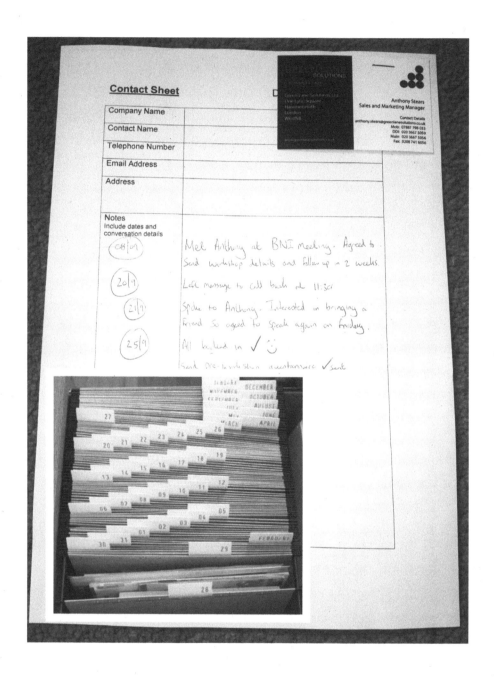

The system is simple and each business card is stapled to an A4 piece of paper where notes can be written and reminders can go (as shown on the picture). You may decide to create a simple contacts form with the company name, address, phone number for those where you haven't collected a business card.

You then need to put that piece of paper (your record), into one of the drop-files. There needs to be a 12 drop-files for each month, and 31 more that are labelled from 1-31. These sit in order of month with the 1-31 files grouped together sitting between the current month and the following one (as shown in the picture). You can then put your "record" into the right drop-file depending on when you have agreed or decided you want to call them back, or send them an email etc.

For those that you agreed to call in 2 weeks time for example, they will go into the file numbered 24, (if it is the 10th today), and if it's one you say you will call in 6 months time they will be put in the appropriate month, and at the beginning of each new month you will need to spread these out amongst the 1-31 files.

As I mentioned above there are some people that this type of system is really good for but please note that you need to open the filing cabinet and pull them out every day, so if you're someone that is likely to forget, then ask someone else in the office to put them on your desk every morning. Where this system can fall down is when you have built up a lot of records and people start calling you before they come up in your diary system and you may have to go hunting for their details. This system also can't be "backed-up".

Spreadsheets – good for those that may be intimidated by complicated looking (official) CRM systems/packages or people that don't have the budget, a spreadsheet is usually free as most of us have windows on our computers and have used spreadsheets before, although more commonly they're used for tables or doing figures.

As on the picture to your right, you will see that the columns and rows lend themselves perfectly to be used as a CRM, and with 95% of clients I worked for in the past, this is what we used.

How you decide to set it up is down to you and what you think would be helpful for your business or sector, but here are the fundamentals that I believe must go in.

You need to have contact information (company name, address, numbers, contact (SDM's), emails) and you will probably find that using a separate column for each will enable you to easily import/export for things like mail merges, or to move it into a "proper" CRM at a later stage.

You also need at least 3 more columns, somewhere you can document and store what the last action was (i.e. sent info, arranged meeting, agreed call back), somewhere to put your

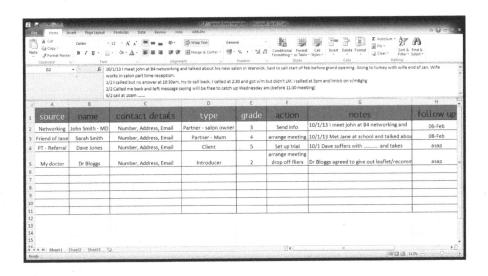

notes every time you speak to them (start each set of notes with the date and just keep writing), and finally a column for a date when you want to follow this up again. This final one is crucial; to have in a separate column as you can then do a "data sort", which allows you to group all your follow ups together so none get missed (this can happen when you get to over 100 contacts).

I like to add in a few extra columns (titles with white text in the diagram), as this enables me to identify trends or monitor activity and success. If you have lots of "introducers" and that is where most of your business comes from, then being able to see which ones give you the most work might helps you to improve your profiling and identify how and where you might find more of the better introducers.

Like the 1-31, there is no reminder and you actually have to open up the spreadsheet and have a look to find out what needs to be done. When there are hundreds of contacts, it can become a bit messy and a colour coded system can help. Unless you're "in the cloud" or use some good IT collaboration software this can only be used by one person at a time otherwise you end up with lots of different versions, and you don't want to annoy people by having 2 different people calling them to tell them the same thing (as it makes you look like you're not very efficient). A spreadsheet can be saved in multiple places so can be backed-up, but this is a manual process so you have to do it yourself, it won't happen automatically.

"Proper" CRM systems – These are software packages designed for storing contact information and everything related to it. They have clever analytics and monitoring, calendar and diary systems which flag up a reminder of what needs to be done at the appropriate time.

Where this system goes wrong is when a client doesn't get given the right training and their lack of confidence or frustration towards it, means that it takes ages to get into the habit of using it regularly and it tends to be short bursts of adding new contacts. Many of these systems can be customised, but until you know what you want and how you're going to want to use it, it's hard to know where to start (far too many CRM companies and respective resellers just give you the generic setup).

There are plenty of systems out there, some of which may link with other technologies within your business like finance and billing software or stock management systems, but standalone ones can be just as effective. You can search "free CRM systems" on Google and lots of results will come up, but "reallysimplesystems" is one that I've used for a client which allows you to have up to 99 contacts before you have to pay (my client opened up a second account when that happened!). Many of the free ones will give you restricted features until you start paying, but you can trial things like Microsoft "Dynamics" for free and give them a test drive.

Paid for systems like "Salesforce" and "ACT" are pretty good in the market and many CRM's now come on a hosted platform and work on the SaaS model (software as a service), so you pay per user per month from £5-£10 per user per month. Very affordable

Note – A CRM system is a business process and you have to WANT to use a CRM system and understand its value to your business before you can implement it, because it will be a culture change for the people in your business. The reason is that they have to use it, and like many of us we like to do things our way, and have a mentality of "if it ain't broke don't fix it", or a "I'll just do it my way, that's what's worked for me in the past." Going through the transistion though, is more than worth the perceived pain, and I cannot stress enough how getting this process into your business will increase your efficiency and help you to effect and monitor sales growth!!

Ok, CRM soap box moment over, but I hope you get the message that "prospect management" is a key part of doing and managing lead generation and the best way to find more sales opportunities.

Self-motivation -

Motivating yourself to make calls

The cliché of "smile while you dial" can make a huge difference to how successful you are on the phone, as smiling releases chemicals (endorphins), that make us feel good and make us happy. Feeling good and happy will come across in your voice (magnified by the fact that you're only using 10% of your communication ability), and as previously stated, this is all the other person on the phone has to go on.

For some people a picture of their family on their desk is enough to make them smile, or perhaps a picture of that perfect holiday or car they really want. It's personal to you, it's what makes YOU happy.   I have an entire "smile wall" in front of me. It's right in front of my face so I can't ignore it. Staying happy and positive is crucial, but it can be hard when you're job is to hit the phone and a bad run of calls quickly makes you feel like no-one wants to talk to you, or you don't seem to be making any progress.

If you're like me and not really a "morning person" then it can help to spend the first few minutes of your day looking for a funny joke or video, as the sooner you start smiling or laughing the quicker those chemicals will be released and the more positive and happy you will feel.

Start easy. It may sound silly but this can work particularly well if you work from home. Start by making a few calls to happy clients, suppliers you like, or even a friend, and just get used to being on the phone. If you can start with a positive call, perhaps asking a new client for a testimonial, or passing on some good news, or even telling the joke you found earlier, it can be a good way to start off positively, and can sometimes make dialling that first prospect on your list, a little less daunting.

You need to feel comfortable and relaxed (though not too relaxed), and in an environment where you can be professional and focused. If you work in an open plan office it can feel like everyone is listening to you and the negative side of us thinks they're waiting for you to say something silly or to laugh at you when you get rejected. If you're the only one in the office making calls this can magnify that feeling, and something I've used is a quiet radio to create some background noise and atmosphere. I use this when I'm at home as it stops it sounding like I'm in a silent office to the person on the other end of the phone, and I find that something upbeat in the background will make me tap my feet without realising. I little sing-along can warm up the vocal cords and it's amazing what the right music can do to your mood and how you feel. As I said, I know someone who uses the Rocky theme tune to "pump him up" just before he arrived to his meeting but for me, the best song to start the day with is U2's "It's a beautiful day". It's uplifting and positive, it makes the hair on the back of my neck stand on end as it builds up and I just want to belt out the words. Go on, try it.

For those working from home you may find a brief car journey or walk, can give you an opportunity to have a sing along in the car or on your iPod, and give you that feeling of "going to work". I have also found that wearing "work clothes" or a suit not only make my posture better (helping me vocally and keeping me in that "work frame of mind"), I also saw a decline in the number of interruptions I was getting from other people in the house, as they know "I'M AT WORK!".

Now, if you can break up the day into calling periods, like 10am-midday and 2pm-4pm (these are good times as this is when people are most likely to be at their desks), and it means you can get on with the other things you need to do (respond to email, deliver your products/services), in the hours in between.

Please note that if you can't call in those periods it doesn't mean you shouldn't call at all. You'll often find that it's when you call first thing in the morning, late in the day or at lunchtime, you have some great chats. Although you won't get hold of as many people you are likely to catch people who will give you their time and not listen properly. Call backs are often scheduled at these times as that's when busy people might be trying to catch up with stuff/admin while it's not too busy in the office.

Giving yourself goals to achieve will often mean that you will persist through moments of frustration, but they do need to be achievable to give you the mind set of "I only need to speak with 5 potential clients and there's a good chance I will find an opportunity." When working for multiple clients at the same time I would just concentrate on get 1 or 2 positive things to happen every day I worked for them. That could be, booking a meeting, sending out more information to people who were interested, or even identifying a future opportunity to go in the pipeline.

If you find yourself getting lucky early (in the first 1-2 calls), you may decide to stop, however you often find that opportunities are like buses and you'll come across 2 or 3 at the same time, and the feeling of success early on can give you a new-found confidence that will come across on the phone, which results in even more success. The reason people don't buy is because of bad timing (they're not ready to buy), but if you go fishing in the right pond and your profiling has identified common issues that your product can solve, then you're more likely to find people that have a need for what you have to offer, and the harder you work and the more calls you make, the luckier you tend to be.

Knowing what the worst that can happen is, could help you conquer your fear. For any company that is making outbound calls, it is your responsibility to screen all of the records you buy (with the intention of calling), against the TPS service (Telephone Preference Service), or the CTPS (Corporate TPS). If you call someone that is registered then they can report you, and, if you keep calling, you will get a £5,000 fine. This tends to happen only when you call people at home, which is becoming more common now that people work from home and use their home phone number. Knowing this is useful, as you may come across someone who becomes very irate when you call, as they have receiving lots of "cold calls" or "sales calls" in a short space of time, and you get the brunt of it.

If someone starts shouting or being aggressive and hostile down the phone saying something like, "I'm sick and tired of getting these bloody calls" then starting with a very sincere apology, you can go on to tell them how they should register with the TPS and how they can get these companies fined £5,000 if they keep calling. It's surprising how this offering of a solution to what they see as a huge annoyance can change their manner towards you. If you shut up after the last line of your explanation of the TPS service they will often calm down and ask why YOU called. Remember you can always back away and just say "I'm so sorry for bothering sir/ madam, I'll leave you to get on with your day". This leads me into what many people find useful and that is **avoiding rejection**.

Avoiding rejection can help stop you feeling beaten up, negative and demotivated when your calls aren't going that well. For me, I try not to leave messages on my first few attempts as it's not very nice when you leave 10 messages and no-one calls you back. You start to get a complex that no one wants to talk to you and if you go on to leave messages 2 or 3, you can start to come across like you're "chasing" or "pestering" someone. It can also increase their reluctance to take your call too. So, when I'm told "sorry, he's not available at the moment can I take some details and I'll ask him to call you back?", I will often say "that would be great.... (slight pause)... but I'm in and out of the office quite a bit at the moment, so at the risk of playing telephone tennis, I may call back when I'm in the office next? Is there a good time when I'm likely to catch him?" They may or may not indicate when it's good to call back, but it stops that bumbling explanation you have to give when they ask what it is about, and means that a half diluted explanation isn't passed to the person you want to speak with. If forced, or on a 3rd or 4th attempt I may leave a very brief message (no more than my name, company and that "my director has asked me to get in touch"), and I would usually play it down and say "If I'm honest, it's not that urgent so if he misses me or I've not heard back, I will try him again next week/on Friday when I'm back in the office." As I would always try to make a note of the persons name I have been speaking with, I will try to finish the call by thanking them personally and end with something like, "have a good day" (little bit American, but it's polite) ☺

As I mentioned, when I'm quizzed about what the call is about I try to keep it as vague as possible, often detaching myself (and the person I'm speaking with), from the importance of the call. I'll say the reason for the call is that "my boss/director has asked me to speak with him and introduce myself". This is then quickly followed up with "it's not urgent, is there a better time to call back?" This concludes things and suggests that you've finished giving your explanation as to what the call is about, and usually leads to them say "hold on a second, I'll just try their line for you".

If you get put through to a voice mail it's worth listening to it as many people give out their mobile (and unless they say "in emergencies please call...") then you can assume that it is ok to call them on that instead. I would always start those calls with "I'm really sorry to call you on the mobile but I got it from your voice mail and was just wondering when might be a good time to catch you?" It's best calling mobiles from your mobile as people are more likely to answer a call from an unknown mobile number than a landline and most of us will often call back any missed calls we receive.

If you **keep getting through to voicemails** then eventually you have to give in and leave a message, but this doesn't mean you need to explain everything about why you are calling and the details of what you want to discuss (e.g. I work for a IT company and we'd like to talk to you about how we might be able to help you", this is very salesy and unlikely to get a response unless you're timing is perfect and the morning they listen to your message their IT goes down). You're better off using a very brief teaser and trying to gain intrigue rather than an understanding. Something like "hi there John, my name is Anthony Stears and I work for ABC over in Basingstoke. It's a bit of a random call really but one of my directors has asked me to get in touch with you, so I was wondering if you could give me a quick call back when you have a few minutes please. My number is 07........ I will be in and out of meetings over the next couple of days so if I miss your call or we don't get to speak by the end of the week, I will give you another quick call on Friday when I'm back in the office. I hope to hear from you soon".

It's usually only when you start leaving message that people will call you back (which is great, obviously), however sometimes the receptionist will just make a note of your name and company, and their curiosity kicks in and prompts them to check you out and call back. I often find that Fridays are the day that most people tend to return the calls they've been meaning to, and although Friday mornings is my favourite time to make calls (as most of us have that Friday feeling), it means you can make flippant comments about "being glad it's nearly the weekend" or "wishing you had more time as you've still got loads to do". This is a good way to get people to relate to you quickly and allows you to gage what kind of mood they're in. This is very effective if done well as it shows an immediate openness and honesty.

Now mirroring people (not copying), can be useful but that doesn't mean if someone is negative and down in the dumps that you have to be too, in fact you need to be as positive as possible as it very easy to turn a negative topic in to a positive conversation.

Sometimes you need to **help people see the silver lining**, so if you're someone that turns up to the station as the train is pulling away, be grateful for the fact you're guaranteed to get a seat while you wait for the next one, and cherish the time you're going to get catching up on emails, returning calls or maybe calling a loved one.

Reward is better than punishment (despite what Mr Christian Grey says! For the 50 shades fans out there!), or sometimes described as the "carrot or stick" debate.

In competitive environments the challenge of competition can help you get the best out of people and as an estate agent, I can remember Thursday evenings where from 5pm - 7pm, you weren't allowed to use your chair UNLESS you had booked an appointment for the mortgage adviser.

For me, a reward is far more motivating and earning my cups of tea and cigarette breaks means I can focus in short bursts and still feel like I'm getting stuff done, without feeling like I am a slave to my work! Getting away from your desk or computer is good for you and having "fresh air breaks" (even if you are smoking!) are good for the soul.

Bonuses and rewards can play an important part in motivating teams and although in some cases you can put a £20 note on the table for the first person to hit an agreed target, money is not the only motivator and as you will often be paying sales people commission, they may well feel more appreciated by a "gift" or a "treat" than cold hard cash. Lunch with the boss or pizza for the office can be a nice touch and remember, a lot of the time, what most people just want is respect, recognition and to feel appreciated.

Being positive will encourage the people around you to be positive too. Sometimes it's hard find but there is a silver lining to every situation, you just have to look for it. This can really help the rapport building process and can turn a negative topic into something positive or funny. Here's an example - With more and more people being effected by redundancy this is a topic that can come up in conversation, so talking about how it must be "nice to spend a bit more time at home with the family", and maybe following it up with "although I imagine that might ware off pretty quickly!! ☺ (in a joking fashion)". Or about it being "great they are able to start-up a new venture/explore an exciting new

> **opportunities". Start by empathising with them, and as you start to point out the silver lining listen to what happens to their mood/voice. Not only does is begin to put a positive spin on a negativity situation but it often moves the conversation on**

The "art" of a perfect follow up call

You should still be following the call structure detailed earlier in the book, however when it comes to follow ups, "the chat" part of the call is where you can put more focus. Here are some simple rules to follow when you're making follow up calls:

Read your notes BEFORE you pick up the phone. You need to refresh your memory and get back up to speed, so you know exactly what happened last time you spoke.

Expect to have been forgotten, and know that "it's OK". You can't be offended if someone doesn't remember you straight away and you have to remember that they've got other things going on that are more important than you and what you're going to offer them.

Get ready to remind them of what you talked about last time or things they told you relating to what you want to discuss, e.g. "when we spoke last time you told me about an existing company you use (getting that objection out the way early), and because you were having issues with X (quality of service, speed of delivery, etc..) YOU SAID to give you a call today if I'd not heard from you." Or if they seem to remember you quickly, perhaps I would use the line, "I'm just calling as promised," often followed by, "I'm not sure if you've had chance to have a look at what I sent you yet (making it ok if they haven't), but I thought I'd give you a quick call to see if there's any immediate questions or bits I can explain in a bit more detail? Have you got a couple of minutes?".

To try and get them to take action you might want to let them know about a special or limited time offer, or perhaps offer a freebie as a demonstration of how good you are and how helpful you try to be (or in exchange for a testimonial or reference). Getting the "tasters" (or "scraps" of work), done as quickly as possible puts you in a position to ask about other areas where you feel you could help. To help increase the urgency on my part, asking if there is anyone else involved in the decision making process can give a genuine reason for you to suggest a meeting to introduce yourself properly and make sure everyone gets their questions answered.

Always be honest and get to the point. Declaring why you are specifically interested in working with them is a nice touch and if you're making an offer (particularly a freebie), you need to be clear of your intention, or that feeling of "what's the catch" starts looming for your prospect. Often by saying something like "let me see if I can fix that little problem we discussed, as it would be a good way for you see just how good we are at what we do", quickly followed up with "and if I'm honest, I'm hoping we'll impress you enough that when you come to reviewing your current supplier or a new project comes up, hopefully you'll get in touch", is quite powerful. Telling someone you're hoping to impress them, as there's an element of "putting your money where your mouth is."

Sometimes when offering a freebie, or when working for a new start up, I may offer my freebie in exchange for "feedback" in the form of a testimonial. I'd still use the line that "I'm hoping by the time it's done I will have impressed you enough that you'll want me to do some more work for you...(small pause).. but I'd be very happy at the end of it just to get your feedback of dealing with us/company name".

If you find that you are **doing far too many freebies**, then explaining this up front can help reduce the number of times people are cheeky in asking for a bit more. Another great tip which also stops people asking for more is to send a bill/invoice for your "freebie" so they can **see the value** of the service you are going to be providing. You want it to be high enough that it looks like they've saved a few quid (and got themselves an expert), but not so much that it will scare them off from wanting to do business with you in the future or even asking you about your fees, as they may make the assumption you're too expensive.

Note for people looking for a job - This approach can be used for finding a job too, particularly if you've been out of work for a while or you are trying to move in to a different area. Asking for a reference in exchange for some work experience is a great way of being given an opportunity and if you can show the employer your passion for the industry or your hunger to learn, AND demonstrate you're happy to "roll up those sleeves" and get stuck in, it's often something they can't say no to. If they don't have a job for you at the end or you've not managed to sweep them off their feet with your dazzling effort, then there is a good chance that you'll be in a position to ask if they know anyone else that might be good for you to work with.

If you don't ask you don't get so this is what I call "**the polite ask**". By asking for something small and showing patience (resisting the temptation to try and sell at them), you will find that many people will give you an opportunity to prove yourself.

Make sure you ask for the right thing. Asking for a seat at the table when they hardly know you is likely to get you lots of no's, but asking for "an opportunity to sit down and introduce yourself properly" or "the chance to come and talk to you about what we've managed to do for others in their sector (people just like them) is a softer approach. This is best asked for when you've manage to find out areas their existing supplier keeps letting them down or falling short (using a negative set of words helps highlight that this is bad, or that it's causing them pain).

It's a bit like rubbing salt in the wounds and as the great Phil M Jones always says, "people are far more likely to change when they're uncomfortable about a "pain", than they are to change for something slightly better or cheaper etc."

If you are pushing for a meeting then be sure not to let it slip out of the pipeline by asking directly "do you want to book it in?" as this is a black and white "yes" or "no" answer. If you ask if someone is "ready" to get something in the diary or asking "if they think it's worth having a meeting?" (knowing you've given them compelling reason to be interested in you), then people are much more likely to say yes. A meeting to explore an opportunity is far more appealing than taking a sales meeting. If asked in this way then the answer can only be "not yet" (rather than a no), and this is the point where you can graciously back away and ask when they think would be a good time to discuss it again. You want to keep these people in your pipeline as you've identified them as having a potential future need, and keeping it "softly softly" makes the whole process more enjoyable for everyone involved. If you have to battle with someone and convince them to do something then you'll probably find they will back out later on down the line, cancelling your meeting or wasting your time with an appointment that's going nowhere.

Always take final responsibility for the next contact even if it is to touch base in 6 months, just to see if anything has changed. The underlying goal of the call is to find out when you will next be speaking with them.

I am aware that my approach is NOT very salesy or aggressive and there is a range of different "closes" you can use to encourage someone to make a decision, although many of them often make the client on the receiving end feel like they've been "led down the garden path" and their words were twisted to a point where they have no choice but to give you the answer YOU want, even if it's something THEY don't. Wants and needs are 2 different things, so concentrate on convincing someone that they're losing out or at a disadvantage by not having your product or service, and in seeing that they need it, they will begin to want it."

CONCLUSION

There are plenty of good sales people out there that do things differently and everyone needs to find their own style. I could be more aggressive but I feel that customer service should always come above the desire to sell. We all have a reputation to maintain and good service today is likely to lead to a returning customer tomorrow, so I believe that focusing on engaging with people and building a pipeline is the best strategy.

Everyone seems to be talking about "engaging with client" but the power of a conversation is far more engaging than the written word, and this is why we still used the expression "they are engaged" when we try to call someone who is already on the phone. Conversations require interaction and they capture your attention, they allow you to deliver emotion, passion and a deeper understanding of the meaning behind your message. So why do so many of us choose to type rather than talk?

Don't get me wrong, you're a fool if you don't use the web to promote your business and using it as part of your marketing mix, however if you're in business and you want to find more customers, the quickest, easiest and cheapest way of doing this is to simply pick up the phone and speak to potential customers.

If you want to find out if your dream client could do with your help, pick up the phone, introduce yourself and ask them!!

We all have our own issues and it is usually just our minds and fears that stop us from reaching our potential. If you believe in what you do, you can position yourself as a pro-active expert. Remember, you have the best USP ever. YOU! So go out there and tell your story to the right people and you'll be amazed at the warm reception you'll get and how many opportunities start to appear.

Words and phrases that can help

Pro-active - you always seem to get a very positive reception when approaching "strategic partner" by talking about you "being pro-active" as everyone wants to feel that they are being pro-active and the opportunity to join forces with someone who is doing the same is not something to be sniffed at.

Opportunity - is a great word that brings excitement and hope in to our minds. By asking for an opportunity to introduce yourself properly, it's a good way to move things forward and get you through the door.

"I wonder if you can help?" - allows you to be honest and gather information. It's a great way to get people to open up as your immediate honesty is often reciprocated.

Saying that you "want to introduce yourself properly" is a great way to stop yourself talking to much and trying to do your whole pitch down the phone. It's a good way of encouraging a meeting after a short time and is a legitimate reason for wanting to go to see someone.

"I feel like I could chat with you for ages" is a nice compliment and combined with the above (wanting to introduce yourself properly) it's can be used if calls are going well pretty earlier on, and you can saying something like "I don't want to take up too much more of your time, but I feel like I could chat with you for ages. I'd love to come and have a coffee and introduce myself properly. I don't suppose you can spare half an hour over the next few weeks?".

ABOUT THE AUTHOR

I am now lucky enough to be delivering my training in a variety of different capacities and get involved in new projects all the time. From Mini Masterclass' as delivered through the Chamber of Commerce and running the "Telemarketing MasterClass" every month, plus working on-site with larger clients is keeping me nice and busy. I'm finding that training that it backed up with a live call demonstration can be really powerful, and is really giving people the confidence to pick up the phone, and the skills to get what they want.

Working with a selection of Sales Trainers and Business Coaches, my training can now be part-funded by clients on the Growth Accelerator program and I'm constantly devising shorter mini masterclass' that are run on-site and tailored specifically for that client's staff and market.

As a member of the local ToastMasters group and the PSA (Professional Speakers Association) I love getting booked for professional speaking gigs. Working with charities, networking groups/organisations, and corporate clients, my aim is to consistently deliver thought-provoking, interactive talks that both motivates and inspires people to take action.

For more information please visit my website at **www.telephoneassassin.co.uk** and do not hesitate to get in touch if you'd like to talk about anything, from how you can join one of my masterclass' or discussing how I might be able to help your company. So please CALL ME on **0800 0087597** or email me at **hello@anthonystears.co.uk**, I'd love to hear from you or anyone you know that might need a little help standing out and getting in front of the right people.

I wanted to leave you with a couple of my favorite quotes:

> *"it's hard to sore like an eagle when you're surrounded by turkeys"*

and

> *"aim for the stars and you'll reach the sky"*